T3-BUX-527

POLLY'S SHOP

Written by Beth Jenkins Grout ✳ **Illustrated by Heidi Chang**

Polly had a shop.

The shop was on the dock.

Polly's shop had lots of things.

But socks were mixed with clocks.

Ducks were mixed with trucks.

Bugs were mixed with rugs.

A girl and her mom came in.

"Where are the socks?" the girl said.

"Here are the bugs and rugs," said Polly.

"Where are the socks?" the girl said.

"Here are the ducks and trucks," said Polly.

"But where are the socks?" the girl said.

"Here are the clocks and here are the socks," said Polly.

A boy and his dad came into the shop.

"Where are the rugs?" the boy said.

"The rugs are under the socks,
   under the clocks, under the ducks,
   under the trucks, and under the bugs."

"Good luck. I'll be on the dock."